SQUEAKY BUM TIME

THE WIT AND WISDOM (AND HAIRDRYER) OF SIR ALEX FERGUSON

COMPILED BY DANIEL TAYLOR

Aurum

First published 2011 by
Aurum Press Limited
7 Greenland Street
London NW1 0ND

www.aurumpress.co.uk

A catalogue record for this book is available from the British Library.

ISBN 978 1 84513 627 7

10 9 8 7 6 5 4 3 2 1

2016 2015 2014 2013 2012 2011

Typeset by M Rules

Printed and bound in Great Britain by Clays Ltd, St Ives plc

CONTENTS

INTRODUCTION

This is an era when football managers are taught to see nothing and say even less. They surround themselves with PR gimmickry and perfumed media assistants. They choose to be bland and churn out formulaic answers that will not stimulate or offend anyone. A dreary protocol saturates press conferences, an acceptance that questions have to be couched in a certain way, and that it is going to be a prosaic experience full of anodyne clichés and predictable answers.

Sir Alex Ferguson is one of the exceptions to the rule. On form, Manchester United's manager is journalistic gold-dust – droll, trenchant and unafraid to voice an opinion. Ferguson prefers to speak in plain English rather than 'over-the-moon-Brian' clichéd football-speak and he has never been scared of saying something in public that other managers would only whisper in private. The man is an inexhaustible source of one-liners, put-downs or, when the mood takes him, long and impassioned homilies about politics, history and the world in general. Ferguson would be the perfect guest for a Fantasy Dinner Party XI, although he would expect only the finest wine. José Mourinho brought him a bottle once. 'It was like bloody paint-stripper,' Ferguson spluttered the following day.

Every Friday we – 'we' being Manchester's football writers – head for United's training ground wondering which Ferguson will turn up. He will often be singing when he comes up the stairs for his weekly press briefing. He might even be waltzing with an imaginary partner, full of banter and levity. But don't bet on it. There are other days when he is wearing a face that says 'Do Not Disturb' – gruff and empurpled, like an officer from the Serious Crime Squad. On those days you know one misplaced word or clumsy question might set off that hair-trigger temper. Yet, even when he is at his most terse and obstreperous, Ferguson will nearly always give us a decent line. Then he will wrap it up and send us on our way, with the classic payoff line 'away and write yer shite.'

What we know is that we are dealing with a man who is unrivalled when it comes to working the media. Ferguson has always known the back pages can be used to his advantage, whether it be motivating players, rousing supporters or cutting down to size one of his many enemies (sometimes all at once). He takes pride in being an agitator and, for the most part, he doesn't care what people think of it. He has played the game, politically, longer and more assiduously than anyone else in football. It has been an epic, anachronistic run, and there is no end in sight just yet. Ask him about it and he will put you right very quickly: 'Retirement is for young people.'

In press conferences you come to realise that, more often than not, he comes armed with what he wants to say. Sometimes he will improvise, but generally he knows what to deliver and when. All it takes is a one-liner and the back pages are instantly cleared for him. 'It's squeaky-bum time,' he told us one spring morning, in the midst of an epic title run-in with Arsenal. Which other manager could come up with a saying that would go on to be immortalised in the Collins English Dictionary? 'Squeaky bum time' is now an accepted part of the football lexicon, regurgitated in that part of every season when the heat of the battle is dangerously close to intolerable. Or, to cite the dictionary definition, 'the tense final stages of a league competition, especially from the point of view of the leaders.'

At other times the whiplash of Ferguson's tongue can be genuinely shocking. Quick, like a cobra strike. Ferguson has stirred Kevin Keegan to a state of apoplexy and provoked Arsène Wenger into a loss of sang-froid. He has put the fear of God in the Football Association and provided more 'slam' and 'blast' back pages than any other manager currently in the business. Nobody has been so consistently quotable. Or so routinely controversial.

But there is much more to Ferguson than that. The soft-focus Ferguson prides himself on being a great raconteur, a man's man, determined to grab life by the balls. He likes to make people laugh and will often send himself up and, in those moments, you absorb every word and remind yourself that time in his company, with the shackles off, is both a privilege and an education.

The mind goes back to that night in Moscow, in 2008, before the Champions League final against Chelsea when Ferguson's demeanour was more like a man arriving for a family barbecue than a manager on the cusp of his single most important match since the turn of the century. 'I love you all,' he cried out, his eyes sparkling, spreading out his arms in the manner of the Pope. 'I have come to spread peace.'

It was not the usual way a manager would address an audience of journalists, television crews, photographers and blazer-wearing UEFA officials. Yet this was Ferguson at his best: warm, charming, convivial and incredibly relaxed, given everything that was at stake. 'I feel good,' he volunteered when he was asked to describe his state of mind. And then he started to twitch his arm exaggeratedly. 'Apart from the shakes, of course . . .'

But there have been other press conferences that last less time than it takes to boil an egg. No doubt you will have heard about the famous 'Hairdryer', the shouting, his ferocity when the bee in his bonnet starts to buzz out of control. It's all true. He's every bit as frightening as is made out. One prick of his temper glands and he will be up, leaning forward, jutting out his forehead, indiscriminately machine-gunning swearwords at someone who has asked or written something he doesn't like. It's the eyes. Those rheumy, pale-green eyes. They stare you down. Your palms begin to sweat. You mouth feels dry, as if you have just swallowed a tablespoon of sawdust. You start to feel pathetically weak. The outburst might last only a few seconds but it always feels so much longer. And you realise you are half-bowing, staring at your feet. It's a degrading experience.

His character can rub against the world like sandpaper sometimes. Ferguson can be tough, uncompromising, a bit of a bastard – a legacy, undoubtedly, of his upbringing in Govan, one of Glasgow's tougher districts.

Essentially, though, Ferguson is a football romantic, a man who loves nothing more than nostalgic reminiscences about the sport that has made his life. Few people in football talk with such rich and colourful language and, for that, we journalists will gratefully cling to his coat-tails. Good 'nannies' (nanny goats: quotes) are the jewels of our trade and Ferguson is the king of the punchy one-liner. Profane and profound, hilarious and humbug. He has become a living Dictionary of Quotations.

Nobody, for example, spoke with greater eloquence after George Best's death. 'George burst on to the scene at a liberated time, with an explosion of music, the Beatles, style, fashion and a freer way of life. He carried the dreams of everyone in the Sixties.

As well as his talent as a fantastic player, what remains in my mind is his courage. I can see him, even now, flying down the wing, riding tackles. He has left us with a million memories and all of them good. The best talent our football has ever produced.'

Then there is the biting Fergie humour (particularly when there are no television cameras around). There was the referee who annoyed him one week. 'That bloody ref,' he volunteered, 'he runs like the hairs in his arse are tied together.' Or the time, a few years back, when United imposed a dress code on their foreign trips for the travelling media. 'You look like a bunch of Bombay moneylenders,' Ferguson brayed. 'Jesus Christ, your mothers wouldn't be proud.'

The mind also goes back to the press conference on the day of his sixty-fifth birthday. 'You haven't got rid of me yet,' he called over his shoulder on the way out. 'No matter how many times you have tried. I'm still here. You lot will all be gone before I am. I'll see you all off.' He might be right, you know. And you can quote me on that.

THE BEAST AND HIS BALL

FERGUSON'S EARLY YEARS AND PLAYING CAREER

Alexander Chapman Ferguson was born in a council house at 357 Shieldhall Road in Glasgow's Govan district on New Year's Eve, 1941 and has always retained great affection for the area. His house in Cheshire is named Fairfields, after the shipyard where his father worked. The first racehorse he registered was Queensland Star, which was the name of one of the ships Alex Snr helped to build.

'I like plenty of echoes of Govan around me,' Ferguson has said, adding: 'I am always slightly baffled by people who are quite happy to lose contact with their roots.' He even has a sign on his office wall at Manchester United's training ground to make it clear. 'AHCUMFIGOVIN' it says in capital letters. 'I come from Govan.' Note: not Glasgow, but Govan.

His playing career included spells at Queen's Park, St Johnstone, Dunfermline Athletic, Falkirk and Ayr United, as well as two years at Rangers, the club he supported as a boy, though he left Ibrox in acrimonious circumstances and has few happy memories. 'No other experience in nearly forty years as a professional player and manager has created a scar comparable with that left by the treatment I received at Rangers,' he has said.

Ferguson often liked to boast he was top scorer at all his clubs. He wasn't. But he was prolific in two ways – the number of goals he scored (222 in 432 games) and the red cards he accumulated in an era when 'you had to

hit someone with an axe to get sent off.'
Ferguson would later christen a lounge at his
Glasgow pub the 'Elbow Room' because of
his particular playing style.

• • •

'They should have a plaque up there, you know.
The Beast was born here.'
Visiting 357 Shieldhall Road 1996

'People say mine was a poor
upbringing. I don't know what they
mean. It was tough, but it wasn't
bloody poor. We maybe didn't have
a TV. We didn't have a car. We didn't
even have a phone. But I thought I
had everything, and I did: I had a
football.' 1991

'When the wind's howling down the Clyde, that's
what forges your character.' 1995

'Someone said to me recently, because I own quite a few horses now, "Have you ever ridden a horse?" I said, "Believe me, there's not many horses in Govan." Only the coal-men and the milkmen had horses to pull their carts. It was only football, football, football. And jumping dykes. That was it.' 2006

'I was one of the Passage 12 gang, and the mentality of being a terrace follower hasn't ever left me.'
On following Glasgow Rangers as a boy 1993

'Sometimes I joke about recognising people's natures in their choice of holiday. Some want to go to Blackpool, others to Spain and some want to go to the moon. I tell myself I identify with that last group. Then I remember the people I was raised among. The great holiday adventure of my childhood was to go to Saltcoats on the Ayrshire coast for the Glasgow Fair fortnight.' 2000

'Many of the boys from Govan who were brought up with me ended up in jail or turned to drink. The temptation to slide into that dead-end existence was all around us.' 2000

'When I worked as a toolmaker in the middle of winter I remember touching the steel first thing in the morning. It's absolutely freezing. You can burn yourself it's so bloody cold. And yet these people built the best ships in the world. You can over-romanticise these things, but they do have a real part to play in forging a person's character.'
Ferguson worked as an apprentice toolmaker when he joined Queens Park at the age of 16 2006

'It's the fifty-fifty balls that make me a striker. You get them, others don't.'
At Dunfermline 1966

'I was never a really dirty player but I do believe a front player has to be hard. I don't think strikers should ever let defenders mess them about.' 1983

'I scored 45 goals in 51 games for Dunfermline one season [1965–66]. Modesty forbids me broadcasting it, of course, but I may have mentioned it to [Ruud] Van Nistelrooy and [Ole Gunnar] Solskjaer. They're fed up of listening to me, in fact.' 2004

'What has happened to diving headers these days? You know, the kind of goals Denis Law, Tommy Lawton, Nat Lofthouse, Dixie Dean and Alex Ferguson used to score.' 2004

'Wee Jimmy Johnstone had a kick at me off the ball, accompanying the blow with a tirade which identified me as a 'big blue-nosed bastard.' It was exactly the initiation I expected.'
On his first experience of playing for Rangers against Celtic in 1967

'During one Old Firm game there were nine bookings in the first half and the senior police officer on duty at the match came into the dressing rooms at the interval with both club chairmen and warned the players that if we didn't calm down we would be inviting a riot.' 2000

'The feeling of rejection and failure when I was discarded by Rangers was a real bad one. Yet, out of that adversity, I found a sense of determination that has shaped my life. I made up my mind then that I would never give in.' 1999

'You were not likely to find Sylvester Stallone, Bruce Willis or Arnold Schwarzenegger in my place, though you might have encountered the odd customer who, single-handed, could have put the three of them to flight.'
On the pub he ran in Govan at the end of his playing career 2000

TAKING ON GODZILLA

MANAGING IN SCOTLAND

At the age of 32, Ferguson became a manager, at East Stirlingshire. The previous season they had finished bottom of the Scottish Second Division, which made them officially the worst team in the country. St Mirren headhunted him after three months and he was in charge at Love Street for almost four years before being sacked for the first and only time in his career. Ferguson then moved to Aberdeen and over the next eight years turned them into the best team in

Scotland. They won the league three times, as well as four Scottish Cups, but the highlight was beating the mighty Real Madrid in the final of the European Cup Winners' Cup in 1983.

• • •

'I remember asking the chairman, Willie Muirhead, if I could have a look at the players' contracts. He took a nervous puff on his cigarette and I knew straight away something was not quite right. It was only when I counted the contracts that I realised he had whittled the playing staff down to eight.'
On his first day at East Stirlingshire 1997

'There is only one way for me – or anybody associated with me – and that's winning. I'm not in this game to be a middle-of-the-road manager or a nearly manager. I'm in it to win everything.'
After taking over St Mirren 1974

'When I was young at St Mirren I once made a substitution after 12 minutes. That changes with the years.' 1997

'They had this one guy at the back and he was absolutely huge. He was built like Godzilla and he was kicking the shit out of one of our strikers. I was watching from the touchline, getting more and more wound up. I got my boots on for the last fifteen minutes and I was going, "Let me at him!" My assistant, big Davie Provan, was pleading with me, "Don't do it, don't. I know what you'll do, I know what you're like." But when you're younger you've got that stupid courage, haven't you? Oh, I was sent off. I went into the dressing room afterwards and told the players, "If anyone ever talks about this I'll find out who it is and I'll fucking kill you."'
On St Mirren's 'friendly' against the Guyana national team, on their 1976 tour of the Caribbean 2006

'I learned a big lesson from that part of my career – because I didn't think I could get the sack.'
On being fired by St Mirren 1984

'Minus 18, on that beach, wind's hitting your face, freezing your knackers off. You never get used to the cold.'
On training at Aberdeen 2003

'I'm not sure anything could surpass it. It elevated the city and the team to a level no one could understand. In essence it was a fairy tale.'
On Aberdeen's victory in the 1983 European Cup Winners' Cup final 1999

'When we got back to the dressing rooms there was a certain air of unreality. There were two Aberdeen rooms in the stadium – one for the players and one for the directors, manager, coach and backroom boys. The players were singing and dancing in their room but our room was surprisingly quiet, as if we couldn't quite believe it – we had just beaten Real Madrid in a European final.' 1985

'I remember buying one round of drinks that came to £90. Unabashed, I simply appended my signature – R.M. McDonald.'
After winning the 1981 Scottish Cup 1985

'History points quite clearly to the fact that to achieve anything in Scottish football you must beat the Old Firm. I would now suggest that to win anything in Scottish football you have to beat Aberdeen and Dundee United.' 1985

'I remember a player I had at Aberdeen, Stuart Kennedy, who would come in every morning and say, "What head has he got on today?" But he didn't say it in front of me, I may tell you.' 2010

'In my time there [Aberdeen] I turned down chances to manage Rangers, Arsenal and Spurs but when the opportunity came to manage Manchester United I could no longer stay in my safe house.' 1992

CHUCKING-OUT TIME

MANCHESTER UNITED – THE EARLY YEARS

'**I** won't be bloody happy unless we win the league,' Ferguson said shortly after taking over from Ron Atkinson at Manchester United in 1987. But his early years at Old Trafford were laced with problems. Ferguson arrived at a stagnating club that had not won the league since 1967, with United's arch-rivals Liverpool firmly established as the dominant force in English football. 'I felt like I was trying to make a silk purse from a sow's ear,' he has since reflected. He also quickly cottoned on that too many of his players had drinking habits more synonymous with a pub team. 'I am running a football club not a drinking club,' he said.

Ferguson's first three years at Old Trafford passed by without a trophy, a run that would see most Premier League managers sacked without so much as a backward glance these days. United's directors have always insisted they never contemplated sacking him but at the end of 1989, in what Ferguson remembers as 'black December', he reached the 'lowest, most desperate point ever in all my years in management.' Many fans had turned against him, crowds were plummeting and a banner was unfurled during one match: 'Three years of excuses and we're still crap – ta-ra Fergie.'

• • •

'I don't mind drink in celebration of a great result. But it had become woven into the fabric of United.' 1992

When a friend asked about the youth policy he had inherited from Ron Atkinson

'What youth policy? He's left me a shower of shit.' 1986

'I need men who are desperate to play for this club. Really there is no point having players whose heart is not in playing for you.'
After transfer-listing Paul McGrath and Norman Whiteside, two of the bigger drinkers 1988

'I am not kidding. This isn't just a job to me. It's a mission. I am deadly serious about it – some people would reckon too serious . . . we will get there. Believe me. And when it happens life will change for Liverpool and everybody else – dramatically.'
On another failed title attempt 1988

'No manager is prepared for the job at Old Trafford. The legend is huge.' 1991

'It hurts, badly. Suicide is the only way to describe our defeat.'
After a 5-1 defeat to Manchester City at Maine Road 1989

'I was as close to putting my head in the oven as I have ever been, and I think there would have been plenty of volunteers to turn on the gas.'
More on the same game 1990

'Every time somebody looks at me I feel I have betrayed that man. You feel as if you have to sneak round corners, feel as if you are some kind of criminal.' 1989

'God works in mysterious ways. Maybe it was the final lesson for us, the ultimate experience in humility and a reminder to our younger players how it feels to have victory snatched away at the moment it seems in your grasp.'
After a late collapse in the league meant United had gone 25 years without the title 1992

'The important thing is that we must not allow ourselves to think that Manchester United's failure to win the league since 1967 is some kind of curse on the club. We must not sink into a slough of despondency, believing that the world is against us, because that way lies defeat and the possibility of submission.' 1992

'I became something of a hermit . . . driven into a self-imposed hiding by the failure. I shut the world outside my door and just felt miserable.' 1993

'You could go through the records and wonder where it all fell apart in a given season, ask why they bought this or that player? What good would that do? It's all history.' 1991

'You can't go into a club and tell people their fitness is terrible, they're bevvying, they're playing too much golf and their ground is filthy.' 1986

'We just don't have the money to go and buy the way we should. So often I have spoken to managers about players and told them I haven't really got any big money . . . They think of United and just burst out laughing. I feel like jumping down the phone and belting them one. It's that frustrating.' 1987

'I would get to the ground and see two directors talking, and there would be a fleeting moment when I would wonder what they were talking about. It's amazing how it can transmit itself to become guilt.' 1992

KNOCKING LIVERPOOL OFF THEIR PERCH

MANCHESTER UNITED – THE TURNAROUND

In January 1990, with the newspapers full of stories that Manchester United might sack Ferguson, they were drawn to play Brian Clough's Nottingham Forest in the third round of the FA Cup. 'Pass the rope' was Ferguson's first thought. But United won thanks to a famous Mark Robins goal and, from that moment, everything clicked. The team won the FA Cup, beating Crystal Palace in a replay, and Ferguson's 'orange-juice heroes' then set about establishing themselves ahead of Liverpool as the major football force in the country.

● ● ●

After United's first title success in 26 years

'You wait a lifetime for a feeling like tonight.' 1993

'It was the day I truly became manager of Manchester United . . . there was a sudden overwhelming realisation that now I was manager of my own destiny.' 1993

'I was playing the 17th hole at Mottram Hall when a total stranger raced up, threw his arms round my neck and told me Oldham had beaten Aston Villa. Manchester United were champions after 26 barren years. I will never forget striding up the 18th fairway. I had a picture in my mind of Arnold Palmer receiving

thunderous acclaim from the hundreds of people lining the final hole at Troon for the Open Championship of 1962. There wasn't even a squirrel applauding me, but it didn't matter because we were champions.'
More on that 1993 title 1997

'When we won the league for the first time I came out the dressing room and said, "I've written three names and put them in an envelope – those are the three players that are going to let us down next season." Of course there was no envelope. And they're all looking and saying, "Well, it's not me!" They're looking at each other, you see. So the next season, I did it again, and Gary Pallister says, "I think one of your names is in there, Boss!" But it was just a challenge to them because dealing with success is not easy, you know.' 2008

'The 1994 team had mental toughness. So many of them. Real tough bastards.' 1999

'A Manchester United player has to want the ball, have the courage to want it. He's a player with imagination. Somebody who sees the bigger picture.' 1995

'At our club you tend to accept that somewhere deep down in the make-up there's something that seems suicidal at times. The players can thrill you and exasperate you at the same time. You're never safe even if you're winning two or three nil. That's the nature of the club and it's not something you can halt. You have to go with the flow. They will take you right to the wire. They will wait until the last minute while I'm on the bench having three heart attacks and contorted with stomach pains.' 1997

'People call these outstanding young stars kids. In a way, I do that myself. But believe me, in football terms they are not kids any more. They deserve to be recognised as senior footballers with Manchester United. They want success and they want it now.'
On the 'Fergie Fledglings' 1996

'There is a terrible amount of jealousy towards this club. I don't know why.' 1997

'Only a fool would deny that, without the series of events triggered by that victory at Forest, the pressure to sack me might eventually have become irresistible.' 2000

1999

. . . AND THE GREATEST TWO MINUTES IN THE HISTORY OF SPORT

In 1997 Ferguson was asked whether Manchester United could become the first club to win the Treble. He shook his head. 'Deep down,' he said, 'I know it would be impossible to win the league, the European Cup and the FA Cup.' Yet within two years Ferguson was stood on a podium at Camp Nou, hoisting the European Cup towards the sky and celebrating an unprecedented feat.

In the previous two weeks United had

confirmed themselves as league champions, as well as beating Newcastle in the FA Cup final, but the 1998-99 season will always be synonymous with that night in Barcelona when Teddy Sheringham and Ole Gunnar Solskjær scored implausibly late goals to turn a 1-0 deficit into a 2-1 win and, shortly after the final whistle, a microphone was thrust towards Ferguson. 'I can't believe it,' he said, his eyes sparkling, a sunrise of a smile crossing his face. 'I can't believe it. Football, eh? Bloody hell! It's been the greatest night of my life.' Of all Ferguson's quotes, this was the sentence with which he will forever be associated.

• • •

'He went into that cauldron as calmly as someone popping round the corner for a newspaper.'

After Paul Scholes's late winner against Inter Milan at San Siro took United into the Champions League semi-finals 1999

'All my life I have based my football creed on passing the ball, possession with rhythm and tempo. For thirty minutes of the first half my ideals were almost totally realised. It was the finest display I have ever had from United.'

After United came back from 2-0 down against Juventus in Turin to win 3-2 and reach the final 1999

'I don't think I could have a higher opinion of any footballer than I already had of the Irishman, but he rose even further in my estimation at the Stadio Delle Alpi. The minute he was booked and out of the final he seemed to redouble his efforts to get the team there. It was the most emphatic display of selflessness I have seen on a football field. Pounding over every blade of grass, competing as if he would rather die of exhaustion than lose he inspired all around him. I felt it was an honour to be associated with such a player.'

On Roy Keane in the same match 1999

'It said something about our season that an appearance in the old showpiece at Wembley could be considered a mere consolation prize.'
On the FA Cup final against Newcastle 1999

'At the end of this game, the European Cup will be only six feet away from you and you'll not even be able to touch it if we lose. And for many of you that will be the closest you will ever get. Don't you dare come back in here without giving your all.'
Ferguson's half-time team-talk in the Champions League final 1999

'I was reminding myself to keep my dignity and to accept that this was not going to be our year after all.'
His thoughts as the final went into extra-time, with Bayern Munich winning 1-0 1999

'It would have been Sir Matt Busby's 90th birthday today, but I think he was up there doing a lot of kicking.'
In the post-match press conference 1000

'All of us associated with the team were blissfully demented. Gary Newbon tried to interview me for television and, I am sure, got a flood of gibberish for his pains. I didn't mind sounding like an idiot though. There was no happier idiot on the planet.'
Reflecting on the 'bloody hell' interview 2000

'Some people say you can't be a great manager until you've won the European Cup. I don't think like that, but it was good to put that one to bed.'
2005

THE MEN IN RED JERSEYS

FERGUSON ON THE PLAYERS

The first footballer Ferguson signed at East Stirlingshire was a goalkeeper from Partick Thistle's reserves. 'Tom Gourlay was useful, had good presence and was utterly fearless,' he remembers. 'He was also a minimum of two stones overweight.'

Since then, Ferguson has worked with all kinds of players – good, bad, indifferent and, in some cases, truly exceptional. 'I've learned that when you miss one, another one will come along. I wanted to buy Paul

Gascoigne when he went to Tottenham, but I got Paul Ince instead. I missed out on Alan Shearer, who went to Blackburn, but then I grasped Eric Cantona. In football, if you miss one but hold your nerve, you'll always get another. And luck is certainly part of it. Bad or good, luck is always a part of life.'

• • •

'David Beckham is Britain's finest striker of a football not because of God-given talent but because he practises with a relentless application that the vast majority of less gifted players wouldn't contemplate.' 1999

'After training he'd always be practising, practising, practising. But his life changed when he met his wife. She's in pop and David's got another image now. He's developed this "fashion thing." I saw his transition to a different person.' 2003

More on Beckham

'You'll never guess what Beckham wore to training today. He had this bloody spingly-spangly tracksuit on – he looked like Gary Glitter!' 2003

'It was a freakish incident. If I tried it 100 or a million times it couldn't happen again. If I could, I would have carried on playing.'
Recounting how he kicked a boot into the face of Beckham during a dressing-room argument 2003

'It is totally out of the question. There is no way we would sell him, or any of our best players.'
Before selling Beckham to Real Madrid 2003

'He is the most precious, skill-blessed player I have ever had in almost twenty years in management . . . the greatest talent I have ever been asked to manage.'
On Ryan Giggs 1993

'I shall always remember my first sight of him, floating over the pitch so effortlessly that you would have sworn his feet weren't touching the ground. He carried his head high and he looked as relaxed and natural on the park as a cocker spaniel chasing a piece of silver paper in the wind. A gold miner who has searched every part of the river or mountain and then suddenly finds himself staring at a nugget could not have found more exhilaration than I did watching Giggs that day.' 2000

'Whether dribbling or sprinting, Ryan can leave the best defenders with twisted blood.' 1997

'If we look after him the right way he is going to be one of the stars of football.'
After signing Cristiano Ronaldo from Sporting Lisbon 2003

'His strokes of artistry put paint on the canvas.'
When Ronaldo was crowned Footballer of the Year 2007

'Courage in football, as in life, comes in many forms. But the courage to continue, no matter how many times he is going to be kicked, identifies Ronaldo. Very few players have that level of courage. Some believe the greatest courage in football is the courage to win the ball. The other kind of courage – and it's a moral courage – is the courage to keep the ball. That's what Ronaldo has. All the great players had it. Best had it, Charlton had it, Cantona: "I'll take the kick. I'll take the injury. But I will keep the ball. I'll beat the bully."' 2008

'I spoke to Luis Figo after we played Madrid. Christ, he wasn't happy. I said, "Hey, the youngest player on our team just nutmegged you . . ."'
Saluting a 21-year-old John O'Shea 2003

'That was a marriage made in hell. The minute [Ruud] Van Nistelrooy signed his new contract it was a certainty he was leaving here. His one idea was to go to Real Madrid.'
On Ruud van Nistelrooy, a prolific striker for Manchester United who left the club after falling out with Ferguson 2008

'If he was an inch taller he'd be the best centre-half in Britain. His father is 6ft 2ins – I'd check the milkman.'
On the 5ft 11ins Gary Neville 1996

'What I know for certain is that I'd rather have Gary Neville in my team than some kind of cold fish.' 2006

'I kept saying, "Will somebody please shoot Didier Drogba?"'
After United had beaten Chelsea to the league title 2007

'Pippo Inzaghi was born in an offside position.'
On Inzaghi, then of Juventus, one of the more prolific strikers in Europe at the time 1997

'Ryan Giggs, Gary Neville and Paul Scholes are the heartbeat of the team. They have all been here since they were 13. They are in their 30s now and I don't think there's another team anywhere that has three players who have been around for getting on 20 years. It's important for a club like United to have a Mancunian heartbeat.' 2006

'One of the best football brains Manchester United have ever had.'
On Scholes 1999

'Wayne is truly blessed. He doesn't just have ability, he has a fire inside him.'
On Wayne Rooney 2005

'They [Scholes and Wayne Rooney] batter the ball in training. Gary Neville was having a piss one day, forty-five yards away by a fence. Scholes whacked him right in the arse.' 2004

'What were you like when you were 19? I was trying to start a workers' revolution in Glasgow. My mother thought I was a Communist.'
After Rooney was substituted in a volatile display for England v Spain 2004

More on Rooney

'He demonstrates great hunger and desire all the time. Without doubt, he is the best 21-year-old I have ever had.' 2006

'When we signed him [Rooney] at 18, everyone said "what will he be like at 21?" Now he's 21, people are saying "what will he be like at 25?" It was always destined to be that way.' 2006

Then Rooney announced he wanted to leave Manchester United amid rumours he may go to Manchester City . . .

'Sometimes you look in a field and you see a cow, and you think it's a better cow than you've got in your own field. And it never really works out that way. It's probably the same cow, or not even as good as your own cow.' 2010

'It was one of the mistakes I made – hopefully I haven't made too many – but that was one.'
On selling Jaap Stam to Lazio in 2001 2010

'Patrick would love to have come here last year, but they wouldn't let him. Players always want to play for a bigger club.'
On Patrick Vieira, the then Arsenal captain 2002

'If I was putting Roy Keane out there to represent Manchester United on a one-against-one basis, we'd win the Derby, the Boat Race and anything else. It's an incredible thing he's got.' 2001

'There isn't a person in the game who has Roy's mental toughness. Patrick Vieira is influential at Arsenal, but he can't compare with Keane in terms of mental strength and pride. Roy is more driven – just when you think he hasn't got anything more, he gives it.' 2003

'When I look at Roy Keane I often see myself. He cares, he's a born winner.' 2004

'Some players cry now in the dressing room; Bryan Robson never used to cry.' 2010

'You only have to study Bryan Robson to discover the right attitude. Isn't he a joy to behold, how he bursts himself to win games? Has there ever been a game he has not tried his utmost to win or given everything?' 1992

'If Norman Whiteside had had one more yard of pace he would have been one of the greatest players ever produced in British football.' 1992

'Paul Gascoigne was the best player of his era in English football. He was a breath of fresh air because he played with a smile, and he played with cunning and aggression – apart from all the great abilities he had, he loved playing and he loved winning.' 2008

'We played Newcastle and they were just bobbing above relegation. My three centre-midfield players were Bryan Robson, Norman Whiteside and Remi Moses. Three very competitive footballers. Great footballers. And he absolutely tore them apart. It ended up with one situation. He nutmegged Remi Moses right in front of me in the dugout, and went up to Remi right after he did it and patted him on the head. And I was out of that dugout, "Get that

little fucking so and so!" And Robbo and Whiteside are chasing up and down the pitch and couldn't get near him . . . after the game, I said to the chairman, "Don't leave here, get on to the chairman of Newcastle, I've gotta get this boy, he's the best I've seen for years and years."'
On his first encounter with Gazza 2008

'I used to have a saying that when a player is at his peak he feels as though he can climb Mount Everest in his slippers. That's what he was like.'
On Paul Ince 1997

'He's a bully, a fucking big-time Charlie.'
On Ince, this time after he had left the club and was playing for Liverpool 1998

'All this "Guvnor" nonsense should have been left in his toy-box.'
On Ince again 1999

'I found him unreachable. Time and again I would have him in my office, attempting to bring home to him the danger that alcohol was doing to his life. He would sit there and just nod in agreement, then walk out the door and carry on as before.'
On Paul McGrath 2000

'Peter [Barnes] was always a bit mixed up. He blamed the game for changing because he didn't fancy the idea of working back as a winger. He totally failed to realise that all the great players have worked. Ruud Gullit works as hard as the rest of his team and they once put a pedometer on Di Stefano and found that he covered more ground than anyone else in the Real Madrid team. Players like Cruyff, George Best and Bobby Charlton went from penalty box to penalty box and I have often wondered why Peter Barnes felt he was different.' 1992

More on Barnes

'I kept hearing about the potential of this guy when I first came to United. Everyone was telling me he had such great potential. But he was 30 years old. It's made me dislike the word "potential" – that's a dangerous word in football.' 2002

'It always amazes me when people say, "All he can do is score goals." It's the most famous quote in football.'
After Manchester United paid Newcastle United seven million pounds for Andy Cole 1995

'He could start a row in an empty house.'
On Dennis Wise 1995

'I wouldn't want to expose my back to him in a hurry.'
On Gordon Strachan 1999

'When [Peter] Schmeichel raises his voice, the walls shudder'. 1999

'He was towering over me and the other players were almost covering their eyes. I'm looking up and thinking, "If he does hit me, I'm dead."'
On a dressing-room argument with Schmeichel 2006

'Of all the many qualities a good team must possess, the supreme essential for me is penetration. And Eric [Cantona] brought the can-opener.' 1996

'If there was ever a player in this world who was made for Manchester United, it was Cantona. I think he had been searching all his life for somebody who looked at him and made him feel that a place was his home. He had travelled around so many countries. But when he came here, he knew: this is my place.' 1998

More on Cantona

'He infected the place. Stuck his chest out, put his collar up and said "Look at me."' 2002

'My abiding memory of Eric will be a pass he produced in a game against Nottingham Forest in January 1993. He received the ball with his back to goal, swivelled, and on the half-turn played a ball into the path of Mark Hughes, who scored our second goal. Oh, the vision of that pass . . . usually, watching from the touchline, I see a pass before the player spots it, but I couldn't see that one.' 1996

'A warrior you could trust with your life.'
On Mark Hughes 1994

'I remember some years ago I asked a young player if he had heard of Denis Law and he said he hadn't. So I shot him.' 2010

'He was a magician on the park. He could have put a size-five football in an egg-cup.'
On Jim Baxter 2006

'See this man? Neither of you two will ever be good enough to lace his boots. Go and get him some toast.'

To Ryan Giggs and Wayne Rooney, while showing the Manchester City legend Ken Barnes around United's training ground 2007

FRIENDS AND FOES (PLUS THE ODD MIND-GAME)

FERGUSON ON MANAGERS

José Mourinho calls him The Boss. Others have used the word 'Godfather.' Ferguson has an active role with the League Managers' Association and has always prided himself on supporting other members of his profession. Yet Ferguson being Ferguson, there have also been long-running feuds with Arsène Wenger, Rafael Benítez and many others.

• • •

'When Paddy [Crerand] introduced me to Sir Matt [Busby] when I was still a player, I was trembling. I was in awe.' 1996

'I'm privileged to have followed Sir Matt because all you have to do is to try and maintain the standards that he set so many years ago.' 1992

'It was as if the king had died. In football terms, the king had died.'
On Jock Stein's death in 1985 2000

More on Stein

'He had the kind of humility that only really great men possess. Not well-known men, genuinely great men. He was one of them.' 1988

'Brian Clough provided ample proof that he was one of British football's greatest managers. That he was almost certainly its rudest is perhaps another distinction he is proud to claim. He is welcome to it.' 2000

'He was certainly full of it, calling me "Boss" and "Big Man" when we had our post-match drink after the first leg. But it would help if his greetings were accompanied by a decent glass of wine. What he gave me was paint-stripper.'
On José Mourinho, then manager of Inter Milan 2009

When Mourinho was Chelsea manager

'I like José. I think he sees himself as the young gunslinger who has come into town to challenge the sheriff who has been around for a while. He has a great sense of humour and there is a devilish wit about him. Don't believe everything you read about mind games. We get on.' 2005

'He has no respect for anyone but himself.'
On Mourinho again 2007

'I think Sven Goran Eriksson would have been a nice easy choice in terms of nothing really happens, does it? He doesn't change anything. He sails along, nobody falls out with him. He comes out and says, "The first half we were good, second half we were not so good. I am very pleased with the result." I think he'd have been all right for United, you know what I mean? The acceptable face.'

On United lining up Eriksson to replace Ferguson when he announced he was going to retire 2003

'I think every coach sees a bit of themselves in Vince Lombardi. He was the great coach of the Green Bay Packers. An obsessed, committed guy – a bit like myself.' 2003

'I saw Brian Kidd as a complex person, often quite insecure, particularly about his health. Managing Blackburn Rovers is very different from managing Manchester United and, deep down, I would have had serious reservations about Brian ever taking charge of United. I suspect that the constant demand for hard, often unpopular decisions would have put an intolerable strain on his temperament.'
On his former assistant 2000

'He's a man who I believe is his own worst enemy, the sort who always had to get his own way. Maybe it was because he'd always known success. Once he'd left Scunthorpe it was silver lining all the way, both as player and manager. His career flew on gossamer wings. But he also gave me the impression that if he didn't get his own way he was liable to pick up his ball and go home.'
On Kevin Keegan 1996

'I think he was an angry man. He must have been disturbed for some reason. I think you have to cut through the venom of it and hopefully he'll reflect and understand what he said was absolutely ridiculous.'
After Liverpool's Rafael Benítez had criticised him 2009

More on Benítez

'I think you should respect a manager. I don't think you'd ever get me doing something like that [criticising him publicly] – you won't. You have to have humility. But he is beyond the pale.' 2009

'It was like meeting the Pope. He came in, hands in pockets, Cagney-fashion, and proceeded to show us all the photographs of Anfield's famous players displayed on the walls. He had a comment to make about each of them: Raich Carter, Dally Duncan, Billy Steele, Steve Bloomer . . . and he described Peter Doherty as the greatest player of all time, blessed with

power, pace, dribbling and control. I was aching to tell him that my father had played with Peter Doherty for Glentoran but I was so in awe I couldn't get the words out.'
On meeting Bill Shankly for the first time at Liverpool 1996

'Shankly was a big inspiration to me. I used to have a cassette of interviews with him reminiscing about the old days. There are some great stories. I remember one at Partick Thistle in the war years with Peter "Ma-ball" McKennan. He was called "Ma-ball" because he took the throw-ins, the free-kicks, everything. That day they get a penalty, Shanks goes to take it and McKennan says, "I take the penalties around here." Shanks just gives him a look and says, "Not fucking today you don't." You can just imagine him saying it, can't you? Like James Cagney!' 2006

'Nobody here thought Mark Hughes would become a manager, never in a million years.'
When Hughes, a former United player, was managing Manchester City 2009

'Gareth Southgate is very naïve. He's just a young manager. We'll have to give him a chance to settle in.'
After Southgate, then the Middlesbrough manager, had accused Cristiano Ronaldo of diving 2006

'One thousand games in purgatory, eh?'
Presenting Dave Bassett with an award for 1,000 matches as a manager 2002

'Looking into his eyes is enough to tell you that you are dealing with somebody who is in command of himself and of his professional domain. Those eyes are sometimes burning with seriousness, sometimes twinkling, sometimes warily assessing you – and always they are alive with intelligence. On top of all his other advantages, he is such a good-looking bastard he makes most of us look like Bela Lugosi.'
On Marcello Lippi, the former Italian national team manager 2000

'He's a novice – and he should keep his opinions to Japanese football.'
On Arsène Wenger 1997

'Arsène Wenger disappoints me when he is reluctant to give credit to Manchester United for what we have achieved. And I don't think his carping has made a good impression on other managers in the Premiership.' 2000

'Arsène Wenger is somebody I'd like to get to know better. People who do know him tell me he is a good man but I don't suppose I'll ever find out myself. He seems to pull the shutters down when you meet him and he never has a drink with you after the game.' 2003

More on Wenger

'Intelligence! They say he's an intelligent man, right? Speaks five languages. I've got a 15-year-old boy from the Ivory Coast who speaks five languages.' 2003

'In the tunnel Wenger was criticising my players, calling them cheats, so I told him to leave them alone and behave himself. He ran at me with his hands raised saying, 'What do you want to do about it?' Not to apologise for the behaviour of the players to another manager is unthinkable. It's a disgrace, but I don't expect Wenger to ever apologise . . . he's that type of person.'

After a particularly bad-tempered match between United and Arsenal 2005

'It's petty. I can't think why he has said it. But I think it's about making him look great again. You know: I'm the great Arsène Wenger!'

After Wenger had suggested Ferguson's team might have an underlying problem with stamina 2007

On Sir Bobby Robson

'I was watching Barcelona on television and when he was interviewed after the match he got quite animated and upset and started waving his arms about. I wondered why, at the age of 63, he was still putting up with that kind of treatment. The answer, of course, is that football is in his blood. Like a drug, he clearly can't give it up. I wonder if I'll ever reach that point?' 1997

TAKING ON THE WORLD

FERGUSON ON THE OPPOSITION

Ferguson usually takes care to be respectful to United's opponents – although not all the time. When Manchester City moved into a new ground, the City of Manchester stadium, he wanted to know of the local football writers what it was like at 'the Temple of Doom.' Then he spotted a City-supporting journalist in the front row and his eyes lit up. The reporter in question was offered headache tablets. 'You've come to see what's going on with the enemy, you little Blue spy?'

• • •

'They are a small club with a small mentality. All they can talk about is Manchester United; they can't get away from it.'
On Manchester City 2009

More on City

'We've got a noisy neighbour. Although you don't like it, they never stop. You know when you've got a noisy neighbour and they keep the radio on all the time? What can you do? You can complain to the council, you can bang on their wall, you can go to their door, but they still keep their music on.
So what do you do? You get used to it.' 2010

'The derby games have taken on a new dimension for me. We got very complacent about the derby a few years back. But we're not bloody complacent about it now.' 2010

'I didn't walk away from the ground after the game, I floated out. It was as if I had been given an injection of one of those stimulant drugs. Instead, all that happened was that I had been caught up in the most exciting football atmosphere I have ever experienced. These Liverpool fans support with passion!'
After his first visit to Anfield to watch the European Cup quarter-final against St Etienne 1977

'I can now understand why a lot of managers have to leave here choking on their own sick, afraid to tell the truth because they've been beaten. We've got a draw today . . . so I can speak the truth. To win here you have to surmount a lot of pressure, a lot of obstacles and it you want to blame the referee, you can't say so. The provocation and intimidation he is under are incredible. To win here is a miracle. That's the biggest handicap coming to this ground . . . every manager who comes here knows about them but has to leave the ground biting his tongue, afraid to say anything because his team have been beaten.'

On being a visiting manager at Anfield 1988

'All our players would acknowledge they were given a boost before a ball was kicked when our opponents turned up looking like a squad of bakers in cream-coloured suits. The sight gave our lads a great lift.'

On Liverpool's choice of attire (the famous cream suits) for the FA Cup final 1996

'My greatest challenge is not what's happening at the moment, my greatest challenge was knocking Liverpool right off their fucking perch. And you can print that.'

In an interview with the *Guardian*, responding to criticism from *Match of the Day*'s Alan Hansen, who had questioned Ferguson's future as United manager after a bad run of results 2002

'Liverpool-Manchester United games are fantastic. It doesn't matter if you were playing tiddlywinks, it would be really competitive.' 2003

'You must be joking. Do I look as if I'm a masochist ready to cut myself? How does relegation sound instead?'
Asked whether Liverpool could end their 17-year wait for a league title 2007

More on Liverpool

'They have always been our main rival. It's always been our derby. Geographically, historically the two cities, the two most successful clubs in Britain. When they get together you expect sparks to fly.' 2009

'They are scrappers who rely on belligerence – we are the better team.'
After Arsenal had won the league 2002

'I think it's obvious Arsenal have been doing deals with the FA for years. Look at the number of times they've got off with charges outside of the fifty-odd sending-offs they have had under [Arsène] Wenger. I think they have been up ten times before the FA and have got off with eight of those. It's remarkable, very remarkable. We hope we win titles without anybody's help.'

Ferguson had to apologise for these comments to avoid an FA disciplinary charge of his own 2003

'What Arsenal players did [at Old Trafford] last season was the worst thing I've seen in this sport. They're a mob – they get away with murder.'

The build-up to Arsenal's visit to United, 2004. The two sets of players had clashed the previous season.

More on Arsenal

'They're the worst losers of all time. They don't know how to lose. Maybe it's just Manchester United. They don't lose many games to other teams.' 2005

When asked whether Arsenal could rival United after moving into the 60,000-capacity Emirates stadium

'Rival United? Arsenal? Never! They will need three stadiums and 33 teams to rival us as a club. Nobody is as big as Manchester United. Nobody ever will be either.' 2006

'They give the impression that lynching would be too good for us.'
On Leeds United 1999

More on Leeds

'I went there once and got caught at some traffic lights near Elland Road. This bunch of supporters, skinheads, twenty or thirty of them, they see me and go "Ferguson!" and start running across the road. The lights are still red. I'm almost shitting myself, they're getting nearer, then the light goes to amber and [impersonation of a tyre-squeal] I'm away!' 2003

'Hell bent on ruining football.'
On Chelsea 2006

'The birds are whistling here and the sparrows are waking up at Stamford Bridge coughing.' 2007

'When you think about the history that Liverpool have got, Chelsea don't compare.' 2007

'There was never any reason for Cristiano to think about leaving other than that thing about people perceiving Real Madrid as galacticos. Or whatever the hell it is they call themselves. They have a pre-conceived notion of themselves at Madrid, don't they? But you couldn't say they were ahead of Manchester United.'
Angered by Real Madrid's attempts to sign Cristiano Ronaldo against United's wishes 2007

'Real have no morals at all. They think they can ride roughshod over everyone but they won't do it with us. In terms of great clubs, Barcelona have far better moral issues than Real Madrid will ever have.'

The same again a year later 2008

'When we sold Gabriel Heinze to Real Madrid we knew it was going to happen because Ronaldo was very close to Heinze. I knew what they were doing. I don't believe they were interested in Heinze – good player, though he is. The endgame was to get Ronaldo. What made it really obscene was that Madrid, as General Franco's club, had a history of being able to get whoever and whatever they wanted, before democracy came to Spain.' 2008

'Do you remember that movie called *I've Got Email* [sic] with Meg Ryan? The wee shop round the corner gets engulfed by the big one owned by Tom Hanks and she can't do anything about it. That's been happening in society for 30 or 40 years; the wee shop gets engulfed by the supermarkets. Well, we don't want to be one of the small shops. I'd bloody hate to think Real Madrid can ride roughshod over us about a player.' 2008

More on Real Madrid trying to sign Cristiano Ronaldo

'You don't think we'd get into a contract with that mob, do you? Jesus Christ. I wouldn't sell them a virus.'

Ronaldo signed later that year 2008

'I love Newcastle, I love that raw passion. I remember being there once and hearing newspaper vendors shouting, "Sensation! Andy Cole toe injury!" Most people use the word sensation for "[John] Major Resigns" or "Aids Spreading Over Country." It's unbelievable.' 1995

More on Newcastle

'They have those fans who are so emotional and fanatical, they expect to win the World Cup.' 2005

'It wouldn't matter if we had Dixie Dean playing for us, it is always a bloody nightmare going there.'
On the hostility of Everton's supporters 2010

SHOOTING FROM THE LIP

THE HAIRDRYER AND OTHER RANTS

Ferguson likes to say he has mellowed with age: 'I'm a pussycat compared to what I used to be like.' But there are still times when he is prepared to take off his coat and roll up his sleeves for a scrap. 'You still have to create a little spark sometimes. If it's in your nature to lose your temper, let it out. Don't keep it bottled up otherwise you end up growling and kicking doors and not getting across what you actually feel. I've thrown more teacups across the dressing room than I can tell you. But as

far as I'm concerned, anger is not a problem.
Losing your temper is OK.'

• • •

'Sometimes I lose my temper, sometimes I don't.
If someone argues with me I have to win the
argument. So I start heading towards them, that's
where the hairdryer comes in. I can't lose an
argument. The manager can never lose an
argument.' 2003

'Everyone knows that for us to get awarded a
penalty we need a certificate from the Pope and
a personal letter from the Queen.'
After Leeds were awarded a spot-kick against United 2001

'When Italians tell me it is pasta I
check under the sauce to make sure.
They're masters of the smokescreen.
They come out with the "English are
so strong, we're terrible in the air, we
can't do this, we can't do that." Then
they beat you 3–0.'
Before a match with Inter Milan 1999

'Manchester United is a perfect vehicle for all the ambitious people in football to have a go at. If someone wants to make a name for themselves, this club provides a perfect target.'
After the FA's chief executive, Mark Palios, backed the banning of Rio Ferdinand for a missed drugs test 2003

'England will never win World Cups. They simply don't have enough people who believe in playing football.' 1995

'He's not fit. I don't think he's fit. It's an indictment of our game that we see referees from abroad are as fit as butcher's dogs. We've got some good referees in our country who are fit. But he wasn't fit. He was actually walking up the pitch after the goal, needing a rest. He was taking thirty seconds to book a player. I think he's taking a rest, writing down the names on his card and taking thirty seconds for a booking. It's ridiculous.'
Ferguson was banned by the FA for two matches for his comments about the referee Alan Wiley 2009

'If you don't like it go and watch Chelsea. Go and see how much it costs for a ticket there.'
After three supporters approached him at Budapest airport and complained he had not done more to oppose Malcolm Glazer's takeover of United 2005

'It was a nice draw for the Spanish and Italians – I think they picked it themselves. The three Italian teams have avoided each other and so have the three Spanish. How do you think that worked out? I can tell you – UEFA don't want us in the final, that's for sure. I don't know why they have given the final to Old Trafford because they don't want us to get there.'

Ferguson was fined 10,000 Swiss francs for his comments about the Champions League draw 2003

'It's a dysfunctional unit. I don't think they know what they are doing, but it will always be that way.'

On the FA's disciplinary department 2010

'We all know about the Doc. He is what he is, a bitter old man.'

On Tommy Docherty, the former Manchester United manager turned media pundit 1992

'One of my players would have to be hit by an axe to get a penalty at the moment.' 2005

'Some players have spent too much time in the treatment room lately. I'm fed up with seeing one or two of them in the treatment room so often and I shall tell them it has to stop. Enough is enough. One of these days they are going to come up the stairs from their dressing room and find a bloody big padlock on the treatment room door.' 1996

'It's strange for a country like Holland to call us arrogant. You are not short of it yourself.'
When a Dutch television journalist accused him of showing a cavalier attitude by resting key players from a Champions League tie against PSV Eindhoven. United had lost 3-1, their heaviest European defeat in six years 2000

'The young boy showed a bit of inexperience but they got him sent off, everyone sprinted towards the referee, they forced him to get his card out. Typical Germans.'

Accusing Bayern Munich's players after Rafael da Silva was shown a red card in a Champions League quarter-final 2010

After *Match of the Day*'s John Motson asked about Roy Keane's disciplinary record following his third red card in fourteen games . . .

'John, you've no right to ask that question. You're out of order. You know full well my ruling on that. Interview finished. I don't want to fucking watch it. Cancel it. Fucking make sure that does not go out. You know the fucking rules here.' 1995

'I remember Gary Lineker, a bright boy from the BBC . . . says I'm childish. Well, he should know about that himself.'

On his long-standing refusal to speak to the BBC 2003

'West Ham's performance was obscene in terms of the effort they put into the match. Even their own manager [Billy Bonds] was at a loss for words to explain. He apologised to me after the game. He was embarrassed that his team had played like Dervishes after being relegated. I know there is a natural envy for Manchester United which often sees opponents raising their game but considering that the Hammers were bottom of the league it was almost criminal.'
On a 1–0 defeat which damaged Manchester United's championship prospects 1992

'[Wayne] Rooney is from Liverpool and everyone from that city has a chip on their shoulder, so if an injustice is done to him on the pitch of course he is going to react.' 2005

After Mark Clattenburg had sent him to the stands during a game at Bolton Wanderers, Ferguson was punished with a £5,000 fine and two-match touchline ban

'Some referees don't like it. They don't like the truth but I just told him how bad he was in the first half.' 2007

Responding to the news that Herbert Fandel had been appointed to referee Sporting Lisbon v United in the Champions League. The German was one of Ferguson's least favourite officials

'Have we got a supply of mogadon?' 2007

'The Premier League is a piece of nonsense. Its introduction this season has done the reputation of the clubs no good whatsoever and it has in fact alienated a great many supporters. I can imagine punters talking in the pubs and asking, "What the hell is going on here, what's it all about, is there anything different in the new set-up except the fancy name?"'
On the Premier League's formation 1992

Exchange during a press interview

Ferguson: 'Five hours' sleep is all I need.'
Interviewer: 'Like Margaret Thatcher?'
Ferguson: 'Don't associate me with that woman.' 2005

'I don't know anyone in the game who has any time for Emlyn Hughes. He is a disappointing character and it is sad that a man who has achieved so much in the game can resort to gutter journalism.' 1992

'I've told him I'm against this war, absolutely. He told me to calm down.'
On Alistair Campbell, Tony Blair's former press secretary 2003

'Yes, you can fuck off and die.'
After Dean Morse, the *Daily Mirror*'s sports editor, asked him if there was any way to improve the relationship between the newspaper and United 2004

'I think Sepp Blatter is in danger, or has reached a point now, where he is being mocked within the game. Whether he's getting too old, I don't know. But things can happen to people in power. Look at some of the despots in Africa.'
On FIFA's president 2008

On Eric Cantona's kung-fu kick on an abusive Crystal Palace supporter in 1995

'I said to the directors, "If that had been me, I'd have probably done exactly the same." They said, "Don't dare say that, don't ever say that. Christ, the press will slaughter you."' 2003

'Jimmy Hill is verbal when it suits him. If there's a prat going around, he's the prat. I'm not interested in Jimmy Hill. Four years ago he wrote us off in the warm-up [against Nottingham Forest in the FA Cup], that's how much he knows about the game. The BBC are dying for us to lose. Everyone is from Liverpool with a Liverpool supporter's flag. They'll be here every time until we lose, that mob – Barry, Bob, Hansen, the lot of them. Liverpool Supporters' Association.'
After Hill described Cantona as 'despicable' for a stamp on the Norwich player John Polston 1994

On the formation of FC United of Manchester, the protest club set up by supporters after Malcolm Glazer's takeover of United

'I wonder how big a United supporter they are. They seem to be promoting or projecting themselves a wee bit. It says more about them than us.' 2005

'You're joking, right? Not interested! Not interested!'
After being asked to comment on FC United's promotion 2006

'We have people coming here to admire the scenery and enjoy their crisps. They sit and admire the stadium, waiting to be entertained as if they were at a musical. We have lots of visitors for whom it's a weekend holiday, and that's no use to me or my players.'
On United's support 1997

'You never know, malaria might hit the camp. We've got to hope something like that happens.'
On Chelsea's thirteen-point lead at the top of the league 2004

'Has any chairman since Mao had more faith in his own opinions than Ken Bates? If laying down the law were an Olympic sport, the Chelsea chief would be staggering under the weight of gold medals.' 2000

'Can anyone tell me why they give referees a watch? It's certainly not for keeping the time.'
After Graham Poll added 'only' three minutes,
United v Everton 1996

'There are some ridiculous friendly fixtures arranged these days. We have seen teams going to Saudi Arabia, Bahrain, New Zealand, Australia, America and, if they could, I'm sure they would like a trip to Timbuktu. I just wonder sometimes whether the FA councillors look to these jaunts as junkets in return for the time and effort they put into the game.' 1992

'David Cameron will fall apart, don't worry. He's not got it.' 2008

'I have nothing to do with agents. I never talk to agents. I don't pick them, I don't employ them and I don't pay them.' 2004

Live on television, when the Sky Sports interviewer Geoff Shreeves asked him after a 1–0 defeat of Chelsea whether the previous week had been the worst of his United reign

'That's absolute bollocks, that. Absolute nonsense.' 2005

'You hope you get a really strong referee in games like this. It was a major game for both clubs and you want a fair referee, you know . . . you want a strong referee, and we didn't get that. I don't know why he got the game. I must say that, when I saw who was refereeing it, I feared the worst.'
Blaming the referee Martin Atkinson for a 2–1 defeat at Chelsea 2011

'Football is the only industry where you can't speak the truth.'
After the FA reacted to Ferguson's criticism of Atkinson by banning him from the touchline for five matches 2011

THE MIDGES AND THE RATS

FERGUSON ON THE MEDIA

The popular perception is that Ferguson dislikes all journalists, whereas the truth is that some of his greatest friends over the years have been in the newspaper industry. That said, press conferences can be tense, joyless affairs. Ferguson has called the modern-day media a 'monster.' He despairs at the number of times he has been written off. Or the way the date of his retirement is always an issue. 'Bloody hell,' he said after one title triumph, 'you lot had me in a Bath chair down on Torquay beach this time last year.'

• • •

'The journalists call this place Colditz. That's right. And that's just the way we like it.'
On United's move to a new training ground in Carrington 2008

'There are some excellent journalists, honest journalists, and respected journalists, but the media has become a monster. They know all the answers, right and wrong. They want exclusive stories and confidential background. They want their cards marked. They want gossip. And believe me, if they don't get it, you're in trouble.' 1997

'You can't accuse footballers of failing society. They are very kind, going to hospitals and seeing kids, but in the main the press don't seem to want to write a good word about them.' 2000

'None of your business! Do I ask if you're still going to those fucking gay clubs?'
After a journalist asked whether he would go to the World Cup 2002

'We're front page, back page, middle page, in the comic strip, the lot. I used to get upset about it but not any longer. There is no point me getting my drawers in a twist about it. It happens, and in a strange way it's fantastic for us that this attention falls on our club. We are the biggest club ever, on the planet, the universe. Remember that.'
At the press conference after Roy Keane had criticised his United team-mates on the club's television channel 2005

To a Sky Sports reporter, Fraser Dainton, for asking about Keane's complaints

'That's you finished at this club.' 2005

'What have you been doing to yourself, you silly old tapdancer?'
Card to John Bean, the former *Daily Express* man, after he had a heart attack early 1990s

'Jesus Christ! Do they get them straight from school these days?'
After the *Daily Star*'s Danny Fullbrook – mid-30s, married with children – introduces himself at one press conference 2005

'You fucking sell your papers and radio shows off the back of this club.'
Banishing the press after reporters raised an issue he had insisted was off the agenda 2003

'It doesn't matter if there's an earthquake in London, if we were drawing 0-0 at Bury in the League Cup there's still a good chance it would find its way on to News at Ten.' 2002

To South Korean journalists

'Do you know that the most perfect English in the world is spoken in Scotland? That's absolutely correct by the way. If you go up to Inverness for a day you will learn how to speak English perfectly.' 2005

'Bayern Munich have a press conference every bloody day. Christ, can you imagine it? I have to summon up every ounce of energy to do it once a week.' 2005

'Never try to read the mind of a madman!'
To journalists guessing his team 1998

'You get my team right and I'll pay for you to have a weekend up in Loch Lomond. But I'll make sure the midges are out.' 2009

'I get the papers every morning and I have a good laugh about them. I get my cup of tea. I look at what you've written. I get an aspirin to make sure I get over it. And then I go about my day's work . . . still laughing.'
A press conference 2006

'Jesus Christ, how do you lot come up with this stuff? It's Korky the Cat, Dennis the Menace stuff. Do you read Lord Snooty? Which comic is it you guys work for these days? Absolutely priceless.'
When asked at the same press conference whether he is interested in signing Darren Bent from Charlton Athletic 2006

'That's a good question. But it would take a whole interview to get it and that's an interview you're never going to fucking get.'
After a reporter asked why United had had a relatively poor season 2002

After United have finished bottom of their group in the Champions League's opening stage, failing to qualify for the first time in ten seasons

'The press have a hatred of Manchester United. Any opportunity and they will have a go at us. Right now, they are trying to fragment the club, the players from the supporters and the supporters from the players. I suppose it goes with the territory, us being a high-profile club, but they go over the top. They make it personal.' 2005

'I don't give any of you credibility, do you know that? You talk about wanting to have an association with people here and you wonder why I don't get on with you? But you're a fucking embarrassment, a real embarrassment. One of these days the door is going to shut on you permanently.'
Another press conference 2005

Telling a Portuguese journalist about his English counterparts

'Did you know that in 1999 they picked David Ginola for the football writers' award? Ginola! We won the Treble that year. In fact, the only thing we didn't win was the Boat Race – and they still gave it to Ginola. Can you believe that?' 2007

'I wouldn't want to blunt your imagination with the facts.'
A press conference 2005

'On you go. I'm not fucking talking to you. He's a fucking great player. Youse are fucking idiots.'
Ending a press conference after journalists asked about Juan Sebastian Veron's form 2003

After Neil Custis from the *Sun* asked about mice on the Old Trafford pitch

'Mice? I don't know about mice but we've got a bloody big problem with rats. And you walked right into that one, son.' 2006

'The Evening Blues? The Manchester Evening Blues? No thanks. Go and interview FC United of Manchester. You've got more chance of getting an interview with the Pope.'
When asked by the *Manchester Evening News* for an interview. Ferguson has always suspected his local newspaper favoured Manchester City 2007

'I read one article that said when I started in management I used to go behind the stand at East Stirlingshire to practice losing my temper. I was going to say you couldn't make it up, but somebody obviously has.' 2007

THE BOY OUT OF GOVAN

FERGUSON ON HIMSELF

The caricature is of a man who could lose his temper over a game of Pooh Sticks. In reality, there are many different sides to Ferguson, and it is not all about the Hairdryer. He has a self-deprecating humour, always looking for the funny line, the comedic anecdote. When he lifts the mask, he assumes a wry detachment that is not always apparent when he is jabbing a finger at his stopwatch, excoriating a fourth official for not giving enough stoppage time.

Ferguson prides himself on being a great storyteller and people meeting him for the first time are often taken aback by his charm and wit. 'The only time I have felt unsettled was in the Queen's company,' he once said. 'There is a certain order about it and you are on your toes.'

• • •

'If I lose control of these multi-millionaires in the dressing room, then I'm dead. So I never lose control. And if anyone steps out of my control, that's them dead.' 2010

'When you start as a manager, what are you thinking about? You're thinking about surviving. You don't want to be a casualty. There's that fear factor right through my life. The fear of failure. It's there, it's always there. Never leaves me.' 2003

'You go into it because it's in the blood. I remember Viv Anderson saying to me that you had to be off your head to want to be a manager. Then I was in the car one day and it came on the radio that Barnsley had appointed Viv as manager. I gave him a call straight away and said: "Who's off their head now?"' 2009

'If footballers think they are above the manager's control, there is only one word to say, "Goodbye."' 1999

'When we go away, there are all the supporters' coaches from places like Dover and Falmouth. I had never even heard of Falmouth. I like that passion. It seeps into you.' 1995

'Apparently I'm allowed to hang my washing on Glasgow Green, which is an interesting one. And if I ever get arrested in the city, I'm entitled to my own cell, which could come in handy at some point.'
On being made a Freeman of Glasgow 1999

'A few years back, when Paul Ince was involved in an incident at Wembley once, I asked him why he got so upset when someone called him black. After all, he frequently referred to me as a Scottish so-and-so, so what was the difference? He told me the Scots aren't a race. Naturally, I had to remind him we are in fact the master race.' 1996

'Once I left Rangers that was it. I don't look at Aberdeen's results either. The only team I look out for now is Benburb, my local junior team.' 2003

'The Scots have always been travellers. They look at people like Carnegie in America and Busby in England and they feel that with a bit of luck they could end up like them. This is especially true in Scotland because every Scot is born a player. The Scots have a wee inferiority complex which makes them all want to do a bit on the football pitch.' 1992

'Sometimes I feel I have known nearly as many scouts as Baden-Powell.' 1999

'Sometimes you have to be cold, clinical and make judgments without compassion, even to a man you know like your own brother.' 1990

'I remember Jock Stein saying, "Always wait until Monday [to talk to the players] so you can give a studied response to a match," but I couldn't do that to save my life.' 1992

More on his temper

'Sometimes I wish it had been with somebody six foot ten. Sometimes it's a small guy, sometimes it's a medium-sized guy. I've no discrimination that way. Sometimes there's guilt. Sometimes you say to yourself, "Why did I do that?"' 2003

'I did look up "bully" in the dictionary once. It said a bully is somebody who preys on the weak – where weak is defined as somebody weaker than the bully. If you look at some of the people I have stood up to over the years – and I have had dust-ups with all sorts of people in that dressing-room – generally speaking they are much, much bigger than me. There is nothing bullying about that.' 2008

'People must recognise that I am not the three-headed monster that I have been portrayed. I've got feelings just like everyone else.' 1992

'We had a young boy get in the England Under-21s. His agent phoned up the next day and said, "I think it's time we sat down for a new contract for the boy." In his mind he thought that demanded a new contract! I said, "Let's see how he plays for Manchester United."'

2009

'Coming up the stairs at Old Trafford recently, a young player, one of the 16-year-olds, called me Alex . . . I said, "Were you at school with me?" He said, "No." I said, "Well, call me Mr Ferguson or Boss." Some of the senior players were drawing desperate faces. They were thinking, "He'll kill him!" . . . "Hi Alex!" Sixteen years of age! Brilliant!' 2000

'We go to the cinema almost every week. Cathy and I go to the early show at around five o'clock. I get my pick-n-mix and my hot dog and ice cream. Cathy says I'm a pig.' 2007

'I told Cathy I had a match but she wasn't having any of it. She said it was a friendly and that I had to help her pack because we're moving house.'
On his wife stopping him attending United's pre-season game at Dunfermline 2007

'I once forgot to get her a Christmas present. I remembered on Christmas Eve and pressed the panic button but it was too late – the shops were shut. So I slipped a cheque in with her card on Christmas Day. Another bummer idea . . . she tore it in two and dropped it in the bin.' 1996

'I've got forty staff who report to me. In fact, I've got more staff than Marks & Spencer!' 2009

'When I was a kid I used to go hunting for pigeons, under bridges, in church steeples and so on. And heights never bothered me. As you get older, maybe on the twenty-fifth storey of a big hotel, you look out and you get dizzy. Age changes you.' 2010

GLORY, GLORY . . . AGAIN

MANCHESTER UNITED IN THE NAUGHTIES

After winning the Treble in 1999 United embarked on another decade of trophies and success, the pinnacle being a May night in 2008 when Chelsea were beaten in a rain-soaked penalty shoot-out and Ferguson lifted the European Cup for a second time.

Ferguson will often complain United should have won the European Cup more often than their three successes. 'We have consistently qualified for the quarters and the semis but we haven't won enough trophies in Europe. Real Madrid have won it nine times, Milan six times and then there are clubs like Bayern Munich and Ajax who have won it four times. For a club like ours, we should definitely have done better.' Note: Ferguson rarely, if ever, mentions five-time winners Liverpool.

• • •

'The nation was warming to us during the build-up to last season's Champions League final. But the warmth was only ever going to be temporary. It's the British culture of being quick to put down people at the top. We're a soft target.' 2000

'The players' pride has got them where they are. But that is the question now. We will have to say to them: Do you want to go on? Do you want to show why you won all those medals? That is the pertinent question.' 2001

'It's getting tickly now – squeaky-bum time, I call it.'
On the end-of-season title race 2003

'Manchester United cannot defend. We just can't play defensively. The fans, the people here, won't stand for it. It's just not United. The club has a kamikaze streak, which in a funny way I rather like.' 2005

'Sometimes we get carried away with our attacking instincts but you may as well die in a glorious way than not.' 2006

'Only true champions come out and show their worth after defeat.'
After being beaten by Arsenal in the league 2006

'To score seven goals in a Champions League tie you think is impossible. The quality of our game was so high that when we scored the second and third goals I was thinking, "This could be something really big here." But even so, I wasn't expecting that.'
After a 7-1 defeat of AS Roma in the Champions League quarter-finals 2007

'The most I earned as a footballer with Rangers was sixty pounds a week and twenty pounds extra during the season. Eighty pounds! Every one of the players in the club now is a multi-millionaire. The thing that's annoying in football at the moment is a lot of mediocre players are being paid very well. Not just at Manchester, you know – I don't have mediocre players.' 2007

After a reporter asked whether he was confident John Terry would miss during the penalty shoot-out which decided the 2008 European Cup

'No, I thought we were done. I thought we were done. When they took their second-last penalty I clasped my hands and I prayed. He nearly saved it, [Edwin] Van der Sar. But once the ball went in I said to myself, "Don't ever pray again."' 2008

EXTRA TIME

FERGUSON ON BOWING OUT

The *Daily Telegraph* has called him 'The Man Who Can't Retire.' Ferguson tried it once and later described it as the biggest mistake of his professional life. In 2002 he was all set to bow out, after 16 years in the job. United had even lined up his successor, Sven Goran Eriksson, but Ferguson changed his mind. 'New Year, it was my sixtieth birthday. We'd been out for dinner with the family, come back, few drinks, I'd gone for a sleep on the couch. Cathy came through. She says, "I've had a chat with the boys. They don't think you should retire. Think you're off your head."' In 2010 Ferguson overtook Sir Matt Busby as the longest-serving manager in United's history.

• • •

Announcing his intention to quit United at the end of his contract in 2002

'I didn't see my sons grow up. Perhaps it is one of the big reasons I am leaving. I hope I can make up for lost time.' 2000

'I'm definitely going. I won't be making any comebacks like singers do. I look at Bobby Robson [still managing Newcastle United at 68] and think, "Good luck to him." But it's a decision me and my family have made. I want to enjoy a lot of other things.' 2000

'I am such a bloody talented guy. I might go into painting or something like that.' 2001

After reversing his decision

'I was worrying about what I was going to do at three o'clock on Saturday afternoons. I just couldn't see myself riding off into the sunset just yet.' 2002

'I'm not going to leave this club as a loser.' 2002

'There are people saying I should hang my boots up. Well, I don't think anyone has the right to say that. It's none of their bloody business. I've every right to work hard and still be here. Some people don't want to work, but I do. I want to work and I will continue working.' 2005

'I'll be in my wheelchair by then. You'll be pushing me up the hill so I can have a game of darts at the British Legion.'
Asked in 2007 whether he will still be manager in 2010

'It's the age when people normally collect their pensions. I'm waiting for the envelope to drop through the door. I'll get my bus pass and heating allowance and after the length of time I've worked I probably deserve them too. But the important thing is that I feel fine. I'm as fresh as can be.'
On turning sixty-five 2006

'I still think I am fifty-eight, you know. Then I see in the papers I am actually sixty-five and I think, "I can't be sixty-five, can I?"' 2007

'Why should I retire? It's easy to retire. I decided to retire a few years ago and I regretted it within days.' 2007

'The big fear is what you would do with yourself. There's too many examples of people who retire and are in their box soon after. Because you're taking away the very thing that makes you alive, that keeps you alive. I remember my dad had his 65th birthday and the Fairfields shipyard gave him a dinner in Glasgow with 400 people there.

The next week my mother phones and said, "Your dad's going in for an X-ray, he has pains in his chest." I said, "It'll be emotion." Well, it was cancer. A week. One week.' 2008

'I don't want to go anywhere. I'm enjoying the company of you gentlemen [the media] too much. Now . . . mark me down as liar of the year.' 2007

Daniel Taylor has been the *Guardian*'s Manchester United correspondent since 2000. This is his second book on Sir Alex Ferguson, having previously published *This Is The One: The Uncut Story of a Football Genius*. He supports Nottingham Forest and brought out his first book, *Deep Into The Forest*, in 2005.

'He's not a football journalist. He looks more like the bass player out of Oasis.'

Sir Alex Ferguson 1998